MOON MIRRORED INDIVISIBLE

PHOENIX POETS
Edited by Srikanth Reddy
Rosa Alcalá, Douglas Kearney &
Katie Peterson, consulting editors

Moon Mirrored Indivisible

FARID MATUK

THE UNIVERSITY OF CHICAGO PRESS
CHICAGO & LONDON

The University of Chicago Press, Chicago 60637
The University of Chicago Press, Ltd., London

Published 2025
Printed in the United States of America

34 33 32 31 30 29 28 27 26 25 1 2 3 4 5

ISBN-13: 978-0-226-84000-0 (paper)
ISBN-13: 978-0-226-84001-7 (e-book)
DOI: https://doi.org/10.7208/chicago/9780226840017.001.0001

Library of Congress Cataloging-in-Publication Data

Names: Matuk, Farid, author.
Title: Moon mirrored indivisible / Farid Matuk.
Description: Chicago ; London : The University of Chicago Press, 2025. | Series: Phoenix Poets | Includes bibliographical references.
Identifiers: LCCN 2024034929 | ISBN 9780226840000 (paperback) | ISBN 9780226840017 (ebook)
Subjects: LCGFT: Poetry.
Classification: LCC PS3613.A87324 M66 2025 | DDC 811/.6—dc23/eng/20240802
LC record available at https://lccn.loc.gov/2024034929

♾ This paper meets the requirements of ANSI/NISO Z39.48-1992 (Permanence of Paper).

CONTENTS

MOON MIRRORED INDIVISIBLE

I.

But I'm closer to you
than you are to yourself
And this, my enemy friend,
Is the definition of distance

FADY JOUDAH

Redolent

I'm alone, I'm told,
And decorated in English script
With eyes available, with no claim to the words

But with flowers on flowers shipped
From Bogotá's savanna
Helping me talk as one of a people

With occasions to mark, viscously rolling
About each other, having forgotten
The mannered European flower code,

The local eucalyptus,
Or bright dogs that range at night,

The ground floor of my position
Holds no dictionary or science
That can really name the flowers

I'm not pointing
Because they're so obviously opening

Even then, trying to stop
Being these people
I'm not alone saying

Back something like "dark
of flowers" or "stones to swallow"

We're not inside the words
No interviews

Against Occupation

after Lindon Barrett

Neither dignity nor the promise
We could write our way into it

If he knew his name and his word
omit the wish
went so quick, his book,

The night his copies arrived,
As he flung it at the wall away from us

He was killed, later, but omit spectacle
So he stays well enough away
And in his wake, I think my task

Is to stop sorting sex from word,
Sex from breath, to sleep despite
The men's reach for my child arousal,
What had been expanding

Exchanged for the compensating
Promise—in healing
Or domination—that I could be present
At all the edges of my body at once

But that's just occupation
Or a grave

I try to talk about parts of this and the student asks,
"How do you know when you're
no longer talking as a person?"

I only know the arc across which he flung the book
Hangs here

Not empty space but a transom
Between life and word,
So that sea trash, arousal, and the whole edge
Of California lift off me

Susceptible yet undivided,
I don't know, but what's seen

And said, what touches, leaving room
Enough to not stick, makes a turn-
Given key in my body, turned away

From the heroics and capital of literature
Left behind or stolen from, not believed in enough

To realize their undoing
As if turning stayed inside the book

As if the outside didn't already involve us
In the arc of every letter cast
And in every word   that would return them

Poem

In the transit, knowledge comes a dust cloud—
Synthetic, inclusive   I'll nod at arriving ideas
Coming down the Jetway—the Pietà trundled over
For mercy

But isn't it mourning?
And you read "encyclopedia" is circling,
Training in a circle made

For "ancestors" we saw mirrors
Looking at people looking away

Like shoppers turning from Diogenes
Who hoped to feel free, jerking off
In the marketplace against privacy owned

Didn't he do that?

◌

From the hills stacked high
Into dust clouds comes our queer air
To strip my high-tech fabrics,
My dour national demeanor

For a love to call a wife   to sit and jerk off for you
In the little chair by the door

But I went to work   Ask me again
And I will be your sculptural reference

To name as foul, as fair, as fictional as men, incapable
And written

Refusing to be countries for each other's graves,
Just eyes trained on the next idea trained

Into a circle for memory fit   to a wrist
I'll be your jewelry part of the past

Doubled Channel Past

To say they'd survived the world flu
To enjoy long shadows in the picnic
In the photograph

His own daughters doting
On my Syrian
Immigrant grandfather were as happy

As children as we are
Thinking of their Andean high desert
Valley and its volcano behind

The light almost trilling
Doubled channel making the paper visible
Not the image

Of his bare ankles on a blanket
Of plenitude laid by girls

Was it a relief outside
With dirt-walled coolness still clinging?

It's easy, you know,
The always told has a numeric value

Then talk of its absence
Till it's hauled all on the page
Counting the inches of air

Between land and country
What's strung on that floating darkness
Through new clouds now coming to me

Off the nearest gulf, moon enough,
Doodling, but no crow

In the actual sky draws a belt 'round these hours
Turning back

Of ancestors
A viral mutation makes a moment
Or a circumference

I steep, catch the eye
Of delivery drivers,
Look at photographs

Writing into the circle
Makes every hour a gentle repetition
Of this wet season

Yielding moth larvae
The wasps waited for

All that time to prepare
To go on walks

To return as a blanket
Of abundance to some patriarch

To stay in the house
To notice the immediate
Expelled

To feel nothing has happened
And suddenly receive
Strange children at the door

Glistering

Young
Clairvoyant body
Inside me
I'm sorry I've been loud
This long, this poorly
Around you   The masc
Worship slide is steep
And never stops
I aged trying
To be at both ends

I dreamt, my transparency,
That you coated my throat
In Clorox from within
A real friend
Knows to stay well enough away
A cover song
Of love seen through
To revolutionary intent
My imitation
Of my poem is my poem
The evil in us
The actual absence of it

The Game

The child's game on our walk
Was to say *Spain* in various intonations and rhythms
We were to respond *France* but with the previous nation's
Effects mimicked precisely so—assigned,
Unoriginal countries—
Disturbing two hawks into flight as we went
"All done," the child said
Of the distance the hawks' eyes
Traveled to get to her

And if in some memory
She knows distance
Is the force holding words together
So that they're free to stay near,
We'll already have ridden away
On near's back, waving goodbye
And welcome, exactly as a people
Coming closer

The Butcher's Fifth Quarter

          If our names
Or the child's song reached
Anonymous graves in the countries we left,
Would their fields of dirt
Listen? No
Position needed, no future
Needed at the susceptible
Horizon behind us
I accept rage
Driven up the nose,
Crevices
Of the whole head, really
And lip and lip, liver
And asshole,
Tonguing
The edge in the glass
That dying opens
But a people
Would trade the butcher's cheap meat
For stones to toss
Through their reflections
          The first is sleep
The second is diligence
Dismissed, the third
And fourth stones are missing
The fifth is having resisted steeping
So casually in pain,
Which is the sixth stone,
That its stench would trigger
No memory
At the seventh,
Drink what water you need

Before it turns
To money, at least
One of the stones
Tends to be last light
The eighth is bedsheets
On the couch,
Any fold a niche opening,
A crevice to carry the voice—
        Stalwart, swallowed, wavering
On the ninth stone we bear you
Out from those countries'
Sanctified plots
Toward us—the orders,
        The orders—
On the tenth stone
Closer to us

Mirror: Distance

STAND APART
TWO

DOUBLED,
WE TURN

II.

it's all somewhere else. no one lives in a country.

ALICE NOTLEY

Closer

If it's freedom or
Sunday morning

Through which the iterations—

> UH-60 Black Hawk
> A-10 Warthog
> C-130E Hercules
> MH-60S Knighthawk
> HC-130J Combat King II
> E-3 Sentry
> E-6B Mercury
> EC-130H Compass Call
> F-4 Phantom
> F-16 Fighting Falcon
> F-22 Raptor
> B-25 Mitchell

—fly closer, a clear sky,
A perfect day

Can be a backdrop unmoved
By any wind

So, who'll take that feeling
With me
Into the critique of feeling?

Before That

I want to talk to you about happiness to stay inside it

But boys displaced by proxy war are falling onto gravel
Outside my window, under the police helicopter's searchlight

The gravel bites through to the knees; the searchlight is a thing
The bars on the window are promised to

And the wisdom of the body, like articulations

Of capital through time, means some things
But not others

The greatest good in feeling, say, or how shitting
To a news video of a beheading loosens my jaw

Nature compels cleanliness

I could aspire to be professional,
Sitting on the toilet and working a little snot

Dry and fine,
Tensile for new figuring like

I'm the god who knows
Mercury shifts shape, not category—

Offal, organic, decorative—

Maybe those are stages of consequence

Tended, the snot worked thin as a pencil mustache
Invites the strangeness of a decorated face

Which blended with certain American things
Like shitting without a video is boring

But where were you born before that?

Free radicals, the Tiqqun collective for one
At a click past imperium turn back

To describe imperium's outlines but not
Their own posed facial stunts

A thing being a position
And its grimacing

I mean I can pair the sass
Of saying "Ultimately,

it's the omnipresence of the new police
that has made the war undetectable"

With a laughter
In the closed set of my laughters,

Each coded to an aspect
And color and digital charm in the pocket

Watching this one, I'm learning
To thicken the line between inner

And outer cop,
To follow a desert's turns

Toward the sun in its shielding waxes
On leaves and with its needles

But where were you born before that?

Forgive me for being so dumb,
With this booger mustache so dark,

Having carried a little blood at the start

I guess if you're taken for a man, the old way
Was to say whatever men say

Louder, so that even dead you're seen

In the distance your words mark and redeem,
Happy among the released

So tutored, so iterated, I might think
Any consoling magic could be an actual turn

But the night sky behaves itself
As ordnance withheld

So that boys married to their own white father
Would lie in bed hardly saying "prepossessed"

Alright, You Light-Headed Fathers

I'd ask for rain
Wait until January because
I'll be born with a sash, this is
Where you shit, this, I'm told,
Is a drawer for aftershave, knowing things—
Systems that churn for hundreds of years—
Earns harrowing honors that get smeared
Some of it sticks, I mean I could
Make believe a thing exists like a pine cone
Opening, but for daddy's spit is it also
The tree's many a small mouth?
I hear of sovereignties, I hear
Of the first world, but having survived
Facing off with the progeny, ancestors,
I'm told, are no prophylactics against it
"In our bodies there are no borders,"
The new AeroMexico ad says
So here come the killers
And their rhetors:
John Bolton
Elliott Abrams
Juan Zarate of
the Foundation
for Defense
of Democracies
Here, I'm told,
is a song—
George Zi-
mmerman
Whose kʌn-
trimən?

Banner & Thrum

Things used
Quicken the heart?

All those public gallons per second

A tip of the jet throttle, a heaven
Of steel pennants

Let's not wallow
In the particulars of that work—sad
Or happy and dignified—

Will those be feelings
And political categories

Because they're diffuse

And determining?

Paddle-leaf flutter trees
Line the air force base

Scraps of light will come to them,
To a people flattered

By our fortitude in the maelstrom
Of art conveying us out ahead

But this desert's thrasher
And goldfinch, the lesser, pull their calls
Out of the noon, leave it

Wordhusk and deader, happy
On the heels of its ensigns

Perfect Day

To stay inside the blind's slat light, words
Would touch paper, a jar, the smell of the laid upon

By foundations, the same steady, wide sunlight

Cut through at the bottom

By busy diesel routes and my citizen skin
Walking around dares beheading

In a recruitment video   Then the outrage comes
To make a story of the tool,

When it's just an iteration of sky

Piled with tactical flight paths

Faithful iterations
By remote control

Partner state

Proxy
Pilot, precandidate

If we're gonna talk about it

Talk of the bed sheets letting go,
Talk of this small house, of the gravel around it

Now feeling like ways for dust to know
Of my reliances, to settle beside

What some German wrote—history is life!

Even if dust describes the space life left
Rising and shuffling down the American street,

Words have made a vector of time
In a way that rounds space into a nest

Wet paper

Or bodies
Are soaking in feelings

We could make stuff up
Or just keep talking; the German meant
The mistakes

Prepossessed

I thought that rote cheers at the passenger gate
For each next fighter jet touching
The borrowed runway

Meant that there's a trace
Of the state inside any moment

Wanting to be approached
With the balance
Point of intention

And reception
Lucid dreamers must have

To thread as shared feeling
Through gelatin

In the eye
—Light's hollows—
An alibi

But now that the sun in the scene
Is setting as in Los Angeles—

Long, thin band of orange
Between purple plains—

It's more as if
Only a thought ago
We'd been carefree

Under the vastest
Of honesties

Show Up

So, we're at the edge
Of this visibility regime?

Maybe two inches back
A little and aging

Against it we're told to repeat
Our dissonance and lack of closure

Scale Up

          Dignified or bruised by looking
At an inflatable swan in my pool
          As large as our times   dares all ancestors
          To scale up

          Desert heat waves folding air forward
And back into a fixed point,   a hold
          On our mothers' adulthood like it's the thing
From which most of time will run away

          The purest gold rings I inherit,
My grandmother's bracelets stamped with the scales of snakes
          We had so much—ideas, tasks that don't really ask for names
To burn in some America's idea of presentness,
          Peeled, cheap rubies from my mother's ring,
Loosely given back to me in a pouch

What inheritance should make me feel terribly
          Enjoined to the bros of first settlement
When every day, still in their dedicated habit
          For one another, men love me,
Asking about my American sentence shapes like barefoot, sweet
          Thing, Proud Boys (no fap),
The *NY Times*? And don't these amount to nothing
          But a people's bad examples

          Of transiting elements?   Now crush the buds
In the old way,   in boiling water,
To make the resin, stretched
          With a friend into thinning sheets from our mouths
And fingers comes a lacquer
          Where we could render any of the pretender gods

Scaled to look small and distant in the layers of polish
And depth the men hoped our treatments
Would lend to local wood

As generously as the phrase "cultivate your power"
Brings news
To each next theater of war,
Resting in my nerve to write about tear gas
By way of drone and the lacquered
Frame of my mirror wanting
To be polished   Now say

"Enjoyable morning"
To have left a nation's bed
Shining, basically
Eagle shaped,
Tasting of a sugar that delays what's sweet
Sorry not sorry
For the dirt on my feet

A Page without a People

Trained to follow after vernacular
American loneliness, I'd pretend

The page was blank
Even as it folds

Into proximities that overwhelm
The fantasy of empty space

With all the potential for plunder
That emptiness implies

Let it imply

The materials,
They're so rarely friends

They're free to fold plunder

And whatever we feel about it
Back into us by the ply

Aug. 2, 1990–Feb. 28, 1991

Well-worn,   resisting a tender regard wherein all else, must else,

or else   a bold slogan carried forth—*burn   this one*—on the spiraling way
of apostrophe—cursed without cause—someone being called

as the placeholder for the conscript   *Try*
and burn this one—flag and word—on a white boy's T-shirt
I read the invitation to come close

So sociable, the sentence—exchanging styles, the sounds and colors
of my face   for his face

pressed into air's ravines, glancing into wind's crevices
packed with foreign   or neighborly dead, else
the local peace

A sentence covers with discretion   already fallen

through the air of having survived men
by engendering, pouring men   into men so   begotten

by just being around—

"in language   we inherit
the voices of the dead," Nathaniel Mackey said,   and where else

if I ask so, having been said so,   blushing, off leash

Did your T-shirt want me to follow?   The sentence hoped
how many would try?   I'm going to sit here all day

in the peace you made and write about it   All the times
and tenses in the sentence—unread, your old T-shirt, alone,

getting dressed, a little morning cold about your shoulder,

walking past, reading the T-shirt, had been inviting, not the T-shirt but the print
will invite,   accepting, going to try,   will have been trying, et cetera

If you have to ask, et cetera, light this one—

fire's vacuum thinking it's the space
the invitation cared to fill   just as a dream hopes that waking life
would listen,   I lean into the promise

in the sentence,   try to survive,   telling you that you are a good man
because you have peaceful energy   The dream   trying to wish this truth
into you   as   one,   incarnate,   as one, representative

but placeholders and conscripts helix through time and tense
This one, volunteer, trying on a sentence   then another, friendly trying

being punished for trying,   did try, will have been
thought to be trying,   inviting,   dressing in a promise doubles
back to will have had nothing   to wear but punishment

Mirror: Punishment

THE HORSE BURNED

IN CLOROX FROM WITHIN

III.

by that
meaning
it is already
said
being said
all along

THERESA HAK KYUNG CHA

Alpha Video Transcripts

YouTube Muscle Stud Verbally Cocky What up there, boy? Name's fuckin Josh. I go by fuckin YoungInCharge. I'm a dominant motherfucker, as you can see, fuckin ripped to the fuckin core, got your fuckin jeans on, yeah, that's what I'ma fuckin 'bout, boy, get on your fuckin ass knees and get ready to see this body get pumped the fuck up, yeah I know you like that shit, lick those abs, bitch, say you're not offended by shit, now fuckin sit back and enjoy the show. These are sixties and that I'm fuckin 'bout to pick up. Let me adjust this lighting. Yeah, there we go. Fuckin lick those veins, boy. I don't think you can, Gary. Was that your name? Is that your name? Is that your fuckin fake-ass name? I want you to lick these abs, Gary. I want you to lick these abs. I really I want you to see the veins. The fuckin vascularity. How fuckin dominant I am. Ugh. Breathe, spit in this boy's mouth.

Video Tryouts for an American Grammar Book

There is no backward Carried in this video light, soldiers are wailing
after scenes of them sleeping With my eyes closing

and with my belief in interiority, I've come to drop off in their sleeping,
their mouths agog, a different video of boys spitting tobacco
onto each other's tongues

The depth from which A video of fields going up in smoke or a video
of the mown grasses? A video of a man sucking another's cock by an ATV,
their long beards orphaned into objects

Voyage to the surface of sleep the soldiers seem to go to a waking video,
a sleeping video expected all the way into its genre

A painted video carries the squeak of boats lurching at their moorings
A video orphans the voice Etel gives to reading her poems A critic returns it

A video of a man's rectum bleeding fast from the mason jar that just broke
inside his full feeling

A video made sacred by the last seven videos

A video of the bleeding or a video of what happens
after his hand reaches to stop the recording A mistake that sees the flesh
the body tries to run from

Men sleeping placidly beneath the river, looking up with both eyes dedicated
to patriarchy is the cardboard cover for a video of men
congratulating men for writing about the ugliness of men

Boots in near unison Analog, benediction, earnest, mimicking
a closed set of faces in a video of a US fighter pilot and me
at the Delta Air Lines gate, his enthusiasm shining as far as the air will take it

A video of me hearing him say "God's work," for where his enthusiasm meets
his enthusiasm for the mission

so that his smiling can go inside himself
in a video of him showing me his flight helmet and oxygen mask I am seeing him

holding his own head in his lap before it goes back in his monogrammed
duffel bag He has only altitude

and the promise of an executioner renouncing hierarchies, a video they think
they make, but I think it

A video of me being used to consent to the conditions Soft mole, hale tunnels,
standing house I narrow into a fine, stretchable line, thin blue, a bright-yellow
edge of least depth, the sound of its going

down the hall A door creaking in a video about the importance of sequencing
senses begins down the hall, so the door will have somewhere to sound, hesitant

or grand, opening onto the bank of the river,
marking an edge to the Motherland of objects, reposed, frayed, remembered
in song You first

The water's fine A technology of
staying, not of staying in place

It's a feeling that lifts I like when you love me
and don't believe in me, even as a video has only altitude

from which it falls back toward its event

Sentences Heard upon Emergent Devotions

Having been called a Mammon, a Baalial,
The devil aspects of dark to whom
You'd dedicate a man in himself,
I happen close enough to consciousness
To taste what words would go to what mouths
Don't call it an ingenious use of the materials
And signs that would carry
This thingly, distributed body
Until imagination abandons leaving
The most basic of men auto-tuned,
Strobe effected, hypnovideo voiced,
Coaching popper huffs to narrow the world
Into something you can swallow
Yourselves down and out,
Recycling piss in perfect loops
Transaction, pleased?
Can you speak? I don't care
Enough to hear you
But I see you receiving this night
And wind, gravel dust and easement lights
Over the safe and private yard
Will you heal?
What do you think you're asking?
You dress me in horns, in tongues
In muscles, you take only one light
From my eyes, you rage
You remember to breathe
You use and wipe and smear   You think
The mountain is rising, decorated in its metals
Your dreams take you into small rooms to cum
The wind finally gets free enough to run
Through you, and you think it rushes at a hillside

That must lift my throne   The raven visits
Always over your left shoulder, and you are so grateful
To be in its downcast, yellow eye

Concentric

Cast under angels, orders
Of drones, of expositors, I don't know who

Or what, if I look up, I might offend
However mannered, the poem dares

Write about the poem
I'm fool enough to say it flattens

And folds heaven's domes into fibers,
Stitched through whatever ear

And out into a commonness,
Something unshrinkable

Being promised us, never
Miniature enough

From minimum, a red mineral
Illuminating the old manuscripts

With pictures and filigree
Through air a voice

Would splice and bind,
Passing for surgery

Circumference

after Edward Kienholz's *Five Car Stud*, 1969–72

A dry winter cuts through poor wool that pills

A little on men who wear their sweatered chests up
A funny old force, it's cold in the desert

Is not the moon under penalty of perjury
Whose axis turns men's chests from hips up in its cold pull

Enpilled in their surveying, their territory they hold
As far as the radius they walk through the Home Depot parking lot

A wave that ends in me, which Eros
Can cozen but not all the way in men

Who think they go white   We hear freight coming
Artists like Kienholz, who take their old shirts and candle-wax

Cars from the Pick Your Part, collect dirt, buy electricity
To sculpt an aura from his installation's calculated facts

That make time for interpreters and feelings

At the spectacle of castration threatening one form sculpted in the car
To be in love with the passenger installed now in a gallery

Is the composition's redolence of time running out from then
In all ways, past a circumference of white vigilante headlights staged

To surround the couple again each time patrons pay for it, the artist
Through the time he made is waving

Off the old shirts and wax and cars to shudder down

I've watched the American news video   I know what I am doing
The men would like priest to be a verb not of the family of Aaron

Pacing the gallery or leaving the big-box store
Projections relay off the men, they priest them despite themselves

They are little dancers like that

I won't come to them like an interpreter   "It is cold" is the report

Of a sounding that is a simple stride across the lot or out of the museum
The video is running in my pocket   The men are pledged glory

I feel forever accompanied   I know
I have a stupid face on the outside

The men can do whatever they want   They won't wake it up

The Great Commitment

after Reno Gold

Gifts for the nerves—the pads of feet wake to dirt   A kiss traps
two mouths   A kiss turns   the words inside in   My friend says a femme's
sexuality is not a death drive   Neither is a masc's, but oh,   how men hail, hail
the mastery of a man's, at every chance among men

And after they lead
And praise
One another,
Having committed
Urges concentrically
To commanding
Households made
In the image
Of the nation
That surrounds them,
The men are dun
They are thick
They are as the dead
And welcomed back

to the point where Botox enters
muscles that would have lifted a scrotal sack,
thrifting cold's reaction

so that the video sex worker   and time—evening, more
likely a furtive morning—slacken in trinity with each next view
to the next same shape

Form & Freight

Porno Clydesdale leadership pony totems

On fire   sons would be   Bid us prance
Tamp this scrub grass to come up   in sparkler light,
Branching into three or four points at the ends, every time

Being no longer a young man, I let my love wear my gold
Italian horn into a New Year's Eve   What do you think

Of such types?   One told my mother that I'd grow to need a horn
Finger the calcium   knob at my cheek   What if
The promise we love is Neptune's white bull in retreat

From a little town back into the waves? Sunday morning's
Quiet that big-box stores honor
By looking away   Embossed on the frame of our mirror

Two long-tailed birds kiss a flower between them
1974 to?   A good chunk before us,   a few presidents

Whatso Goes

Whatso goes having leaned to sex from me
To a nation's ears runs back as the plangency

Ringing from what goods or boys such a curious people
Might hope to chamber, and one I knew if he cared to hold

What he saw of me trying what type—
Young thing without being severe

Therein delicate clappers strike wet the sides
Of what words—nut and pig, spit and rim, pastoral heritage hills

Speak usefully, believe in beauty knowing our values   Silent,
His eyes coached once which white to follow

From the sauna to the stalls   Anonymous, learning
We sat in steam not choosing each other

Until we allowed, wherein did go what words that lead my cum
Urgently onto his thigh, having learned to want

To be young things in a continuous tense
Knowing who to follow to lay there a path

Outside, to ride on dry air over freedom wrung out
In the cant of its advocates, expositors

He knew, I think, sitting apart we were things and labor
Dissolved together, our salty peasantries

Would sound that chamber's nadir

Thirst Petition

I'll borrow a flower code cut down
To the eloquence of irises

For my mother, the Semitic ghost in white skin
Among certain continental American things—

The paved streets; modern, integrated men; feelings

Contracted; and nothing but parking lot trees to shed their bark
Above the graves of women, guiding their shades

Toward the flower's namesake goddess who puts to sleep
Those who perjure, daughter of Thaumas

And the cloud nymph Electra,
Is this what it is
To be raced at the end of a long line of pricks? Iris,

I open my mouth

Under your ewer pouring the Styx

To One's Honor

"It's true"   our trained

Builders say of   something without
Flourishes or   deviation

Fixed to one's   honor my
Rumor   hearsay
And wishes to   the things I a

Weedy thing   says right at
The edge of   our ages

There's a circle a   minute folds space while

Real   weather
The calendar   and the bamboo

Stand in a   desert spring
Gray and green and   turn in time and
The heat it brings   a next or first

Violation   of me at nine
Or twenty-   seven so
That thereafter my   necessarily

Welcomed fear   makes a room
And puts me   in it where

A little simple   pornography calms
Me right down takes up   the space well enough
And the chanted   fucking is like
Exquisitely formal   transubstantiation

I look up   to address
A neutral   kind of shame

And its a-   wareness lays
A gentle hand   on my sternum

Receives or takes?

It's just a hand

One guesses one is asking
about the hand's verb

One can't know
what the other one
does under one's hand

What does one
want to know?

If after   the speaking
The ears can   admit things

Again the   sounds of breath
With the ghost always   of the ghost body
From which they came   think of a place

Without reading   the words sex was
Sloughing   off of
The child to   say I was

Leaking some   release of
Awareness   in water

As rain   falling

Down the   year Who

Is soaking in   all this paper?
Folded space   it's really

Very small   no feeling

Need be there with   me I'm putting
The words in   someone to look

At as I am   looking to be
Where words just make   another room

Come 'round   come rain
Hand   here

Having Already Been Said

Wanting to be seen as a touch

Shallow the light   about the breaths
Confederated   the light
Powders dust   an accent
Faces forward   into a whole downtown meeting house

Surety   that bearing

Behind us   the air laden with our sloughed bits
Warmths we dance about as young things

Love holes out a face
In our mouths   the certain love

What did you say I'll say?

Mirror: Say

A HEAVEN
OF STEEL PENNANTS

A HAVEN OF
STOLEN PENANCE

IV.

For those who, set low, would cast themselves lower
through the mirror the sky is.

A Movie Called Mimesis

Thinnest sliver
Of new moonlight

At the horn tips of mule deer
Turned toward us

Their dark eyes don't know
Our dry heels imitate the mountains

"Women imitate the earth"

House finches, quaking,
Imitate chambers

Like Daniel's prints saying *freedom*

without love posted at the outskirts,
Men wield mirrors at men,

Making of each the other's baby,
Spun 'round,

While the rest of us stay in bed

And in our closed eyes sense the touch
Of light is a given to use
If we feel like it

We will get up
In a movie about us

We'll go to a lower desert,
Only the thinnest air in our way

Released, certain moods will flare

Our mouths saying,
"You don't get too precious"

Like things are very small, really

They just turn over
And get lost

Across several versions of the portrait
Ragged edged, the mirror's
Useful mercury,

Sonorous behind the glass, almost a return
Before first light assembles the blue

Then what can we tell?

That we took an accent

From a dialect that never made it
Down the mountains?

That we know how to get thin

And turn, saying, "I'm not
really interested in my affect"?

However mannered,
          "Uh-huh,"
The poem says back

Moon Mirrored Indivisible

In the mirror I've said, "Immigrant
my name is argument,
as small as my means"

As weakly as the moon reflecting
The gravity of stars
Trying to unearth ancient *huacos*—vessels
For gods

Who otherwise inhabit local boulders,
Traffic circles, the Circle K,
But I've been dreaming

Of killer ghosts to be dealt with
In real-time ways like
        breathe in, hold,

        turn away—blood
        on my face
        and shirt and hands—

From a wayward truth about great ancestors

"They're damaged, they're damaged,
they're so
comfortable," said

In a three-line English
That should help me wash
The present moment of belief, this

On a day without gods,
With only the staff they offered us to strike Earth
And there make the navel of the world

Don't even bother to break it

Magnificat Mirror Petition

As a mirror fears the seen
But travels in them
I look for eyes fierce enough
To move a love into me as far

As Mother Mary's Magnificat
Would teach me to carry a man's world
The other way out

"He has filled the hungry with good things"

Say this poem already slanders
And begs, sucks teeth
And claps loud, as it carries us
Through the yard to the pool

All I see is dust and trees, an idea of death
Or the ghost of owning
Strung through rain, soft

In the motion sensor light
And I'm sorry, because I'm happy, I filter
The smaller waters through,

Piling them into words
That petition for a little elegance,

For my ass to bend to the wind
Coming off the pool water, so when I stand,
I stand in a long line of filled bodies

What we bear is the horse burned
In Pennsylvania

White boys poured accelerant on its back and neck
And set the match to no allegory, all matter

No longer a plane of flights, a plane of movement,
A plane of kinetic aptitude, of kinetic feeling

Put the pity there to stand
In for those who think they're magnified enough
To lope outside the reflection

Not born free but released,
The ghost of the horse
On fire is the slowest thing

Making its own physics
That comes with its own laws

Be thou gentle,

Refined
In bearing

Exvocation

My ghost story is just a voice, so close
At my ear that its pushed air, not its words,
Woke me to an empty bedside

But the Internet has a boy child of faith
Pressing up to kiss the pope

On the mouth, photographed circa 1980
With every near problem of that scene
Wholly pressed onto that scene

It won't be a story unless I make it that
With words being mirrors

And the transit back through their reflections,
The ear couldn't be the mind's
It's the outside's

And the outside curves involutedly
To kiss my eyelids,
The cheapest meat

Over eyes trying to see at the speed
That things invite me to see,
Available to be judged

By feel more than by faith,
The child can leave the photo

But the gesture stays like a tunnel stays
After shuttling the idea of a people
Into the fact of its nearest mouth

If we fall back out like drops of rain
Distant, repeating,
We might seem a river

But we'll be close enough to pull all ears,
All breath out on the air of our scream

Arts & Craft

I know what I'm going to do next, and I know
What I'm going to trace
            Stone moon,
Broken ship,
            And the cloud that's landing
If my mother was the femme in our story,
Raising me with her sister, the butch,
Then whoso frees whatever masc they want
From men is already king
But I'll torch my energetic sadness, pouring up
To burn the air between body and country
Like the mosquito in its fancy stripes
Trying to bite through my jeans
The doves have been so angry
And horny in their cups
Or in the sky's domed cup of the season
Around this house with friends who are saying goodnight
From faces that have already been free and leaving,
Taking corners slowly, greasy skids
Going down to the same ditch of solace
Like our kid said petitioning her way into our bed,
I just want to lie here like a number

Meaning the many and the shape
Seen from above when we're going
With the animals in the transiting black air
Hummingbirds all over this early June
Aren't war gods because they startle my instruments,
Extending only so far into the layered resin
Darkness the park dogs howl in
To call nearer ghosts who look for a sudden give
In our future, like playing
At our daughter's pretend deathbed
This morning, she wanted me to be a theater
Resounding last words of advice
We glued flakes from the pearlescent edge
Of the nautilus shell to imagine all the folds
And surface strain of a sail triangling forth
The ark she outlined to take her

In the story my mother worked
For a military dictatorship's ministry
Of health, a sisterhood of clerks
Amid "how handsome, the officers"
And when she chose to have me,
I was born or let go as she screamed
Her mother's name, bursting
The thinnest capillaries, purple
About her neck—that screaming,
To touch air without breath
At the edges of the words
Along which any point is creation,
Folds a path that doubles back
To what home?
The river can be a border
Or the reason for a city,
A place for mass burials in the first days of a coup
We drink the Euphrates, the Mapocho
In a thirst that tracks to no writ,
No guarantee of a systemic critique when everything
And a people need critiques by many and many
An elegant hand

When the fascists need to get silly
Off themselves—no pretending—
They parade in boats, they dance
At the rally to whatever's playing,
They tighten their faces
Everyone knows the truth
All the time
It's beautiful like that, abiding,
Immovable, common
Fady says that Darwish said,
"No people are smaller than their poem"
Say it again
When they come to ask
—Rigor, value, coinage—
Mouthfuls, heavy enough to think we're here
My child's fitful, hard words in her sleep
The quiet that follows
The state's circling planes
Long avenues and different drugs
To meet the moment, not yet dangerous
Or disposable enough to kill or disappear

“Revolution finds a way,” Tongo says
“You guys are negative,” Jane says through
Wind chimes tuned to the golden ratio
We should go
Into a slight band of teal in the sky,
Light the trash fire and palm fronds
Under the new form serpent wending down
To bring air onto Earth, stars onto my eyes
Strung to my belly lines, the gifts—
The rain in rivers
Given to real estate for graves
Cold fingers, gold breastplate
As sure as I wear my grandmother’s cross
I drop the amulet, peeled
Black air turning somewhere in a cave
Pisces wheeling through dream’s black water,
While Venus goes to my mother Taurus
Let the bull eat good grass, drink wet water
Frame my favorite photograph of her
A document says itself
Plus an effluence of time waving
Us back along geometries that adorned
The old vessels with the shapes of the rooms
We’ll come to pour out of

I've been a child surrounded
I've been a fiction talking, a state flower signaling,
A monstrance filled by everyone not-a-man,
Casting shadows at my eastern wall
In the work of adding one another in time
I see an actual cricket turned gray, clung to the corner's web
In its deathful leaving and still
My daughter declares that I teach her nothing's real
Not knowing how to look for her,
I thought the picture held an eye to see with
But it's a whole head ringing
We send her away with ideas
We take a walk sick with finery,
Seeing all the hill grass blown north,
And she asks, "Why are you so angry?"
Pretender gods, gods of leaving

Everything runs ahead
A story promises that I'll catch up
But a voice that's stretching into the words,
So warm, not asking for anything,
Drafts above mother of the sanitation plant,
Mother of the second queen,
Mother of the trees the new hive
Will visit on their way
As quantity, extension, inhalation
Of the fabric that folds
Love inside and outside at once,
Along a transference between atomic poles
That's transgenerational because it got here

Onto the page where I try to write
About my grandmother's first pregnancy
She was an Aleppo daughter ordered from a bride book,
Bringing the wrong language to the Andes
Her new stepkids took her first stillborn by the heel,
Far from her Arabic, taunting

I heard the story as a child, not told to me
But strung up in the air around me

That distance from her body to her fetus,
My friends tell me, would be called *massafa* in Arabic
But she might say it's *bu'd*—a whole dimension

Where both the story
And the state break a little,
Dicks are just more of the porous
Surface on the folding river running tense
Enough for anyone to walk on
Or soft releasing the dead
From their shapes; they come nearer
Inside, an increase that wants to turn out
More accountable than each other's healers
Or comrades,
To train a love for whoever, in their gesture
And trace, would help us make of poems
A resonance not lonely or owned,
Opening at each heel's step to sense
One another having gone before

Practicing how to vacate detachment and still
Rightly unwelcomed in the words,
I pronounce whatever comes my conviction
I know that the horse wading in to soak
Holds me in the dream water
By letting me see it, I know that when I fill
With breath enough to float
And fold into those already here,
Every inch of altitude surprises,
Falling into the mirror the sky is

The Moon in Cancer

Run down, or risen
Far enough to catch the moon's reach

For trees aglow with chlorine
From the pool in their leaves and garlands

Left over from a long-gone national holiday
That wants me

To wake up awake, holding on
To which expectation just ahead?

        If you have to ask, moon child,
        You're already glowing

Your silver face and our only friends in the sky,
The doddering in their eyes

Looking down to this pool deck,
Barrel cactus, pink gravel   Having been seen

Comes with its own annotations

I'll go to sleep
Asleep

Unwelcomed but held
By a word just behind

Crease

I know everyone wanted

Their stupid church high on a hill, but my favorite things—

Happy things that I thought   drifting down into sleep   and all the day's faces

That afflict—set low, I could be the paper

Their words ravish or remember

And the end of their script

But if the actual horse on fire   and its event out of these words

Fallen and gathered back through love,
Trying not   to be with but of,

Fold into petals around the trace of that touch,

I'll be of a people

Who concentrate on sex and sense and artifice like that

To crease closer the outside's infinite regress

So that dying,

Actual dying,   only brings us into the next fold   about a flower thrown

After a life unafraid, no smaller than our poem

Mirror: Arc

HE CAST THE BOOK
THE ARC ACROSS WHICH

THE ARK SHE OUTLINED
TO TAKE HER

ACKNOWLEDGMENTS

I am grateful to the editors and publishers of the following journals and projects, in which earlier versions of these poems first appeared:

Berkeley Poetry Review: "Poem"
Bomb Magazine: "Aug. 2, 1990–Feb. 28, 1991"; "Glistering"
Brooklyn Rail: "Redolent"; "Scale Up"; "Sentences Heard upon Emergent Devotions" (as "Sentences upon Emergent Devotions"); "Video Tryouts for an American Grammar Book"
Here to Stay (HarperCollins): "Video Tryouts for an American Grammar Book"
Jewish Currents: "Closer"
Lana Turner Journal: "Doubled Channel Past"; "The Game" (as "Henequen Yarn Song Begun for Ángel Dominguez on Their Birthday"); "A Page without a People"; "Concentric"; "The Great Commitment"; "Whatso Goes"; "Thirst Petition"
Paris Review: "Crease"
poets.org/Poem-a-Day (Academy of American Poets): "The Butcher's Fifth Quarter"; "A Movie Called Mimesis" (as "Mimesis")
Poetry: "Moon Mirrored Indivisible"
A Public Space: "Prepossessed"
Redolent, with artist Nancy Friedemann-Sánchez (Singing Saw Press): "Alright, You Light-Headed Fathers"; "Arts & Craft"; "Redolent"; "Scale Up"; "Exvocation" (as "Rain Transit")
The Tiny: "Alright, You Light-Headed Fathers"; "Redolent"

Thank you to Susan Briante and Gianna for the distance and for the folding back.

Thank you to all the poets and friends, living and dead, whose work and company help me. I'm lucky to write alongside you. Special thanks to Susan Briante, Hayan Charara, Jos Charles, Anthony Cody, Ángel Dominguez, Carolina Ebeid, Carmen Giménez, Valyntina Grenier, Marwa Helal, Fady Joudah, Phil Metres, Jane Miller, Brandon Shimoda, and Dare Williams, for their notes and dialogue.

I'm grateful for residencies from the Headlands Center for the Arts, for a visiting Holloway Lectureship in the Practice of Poetry at the University of California, Berkeley, and for the USA Fellowship from United States Artists, all of which provided time, affirmation, and community.

Thank you to the scholars and artists in the Desert Futures collective, especially Doyle David Calhoun, Suban Nur Cooley, Jill Jarvis, Argyro Nicolaou, Eda Pepi, Francisco Robles, and Teresa Villa-Ignacio, as well as to the folks at rile* bookshop and project space in Brussels and especially Filip Jakab, for including me in conversations that helped me find a way through this book.

For seeing what this book was and what it could be, my thanks go to the team at the University of Chicago Press, including David B. Olsen, Lily Sadowsky, and the Phoenix Poets series editors Rosa Alcalá, Doug Kearney, Katie Peterson, and Srikanth Reddy.

NOTES ON THE TEXT

I.

Covering "Dambala," originally by the Bahamian singer-songwriter Exuma, Nina Simone sang, "You slavers will know what it's / Like to be a slave / Slave to your mind / Slave to your race / You won't go to heaven / You won't go to hell / You'll remain in your graves / With the stench and the smell." Lindon Barrett lived and died so as to always stay but never stay in place.

"Poem" is for Susan Briante.

"The Game" is for Ángel Dominguez.

"The fifth quarter" is a term used in parts of Italy for the supposedly undesirable leftover cuts of meat sold at the cheapest prices.

The "Mirror" poems follow the work of artist Na Mira, specifically *Tetraphobia*, 2022, 16 mm film transfer and 2-channel infrared HD video, sound, black mirror, 20:24, looped, 16 × 10.5 × 8 feet, Company Gallery, New York, exhibited at the Museum of Contemporary Art in Tucson in 2023.

Traced back to its Proto-Indo-European root, the prefix *dis-*, as in *distance*, becomes *bis-*, as in *two*.

II.

Throughout the book *America* and *American* refer to the School of the Americas, which trained torturers in the 1980s; to the South American elites who used their

Ivy League educations to privatize national economies during the 1990s; and to the t-shirt that reads "Pinochet did nothing wrong," popular with the global far right in the twenty-first century. By these terms I mean bell hook's formulation "white supremacist capitalist patriarchy," realized on a hemispheric scale—a coherent and reciprocal (if asymmetrical) network that attempts to hide behind practices of resistance, behind regional and cultural particulars, behind diasporic identities sometimes referred to collectively as Latinidad.

Under torture in US custody, Khalid Sheikh Mohammed confessed to orchestrating the videotaped beheading of US journalist Daniel Pearl in Pakistan in 2002. The so-called Islamic State followed with its own videotaped beheadings in 2014–15, including that of US journalist James Foley.

Researcher Sue Tait identified a shift occurring during the height of the Second Gulf War, around 2005, in which the site Ogrish.com went from being a niche for gore to being a purveyor of newsworthy and moralistic video content, feeding legacy news organizations in the United States and United Kingdom. See Tait, "Pornographies of Violence? Internet Spectatorship on Body Horror," *Critical Studies in Media Communication* 25, no. 1 (March 2008): 91–111.

I lift the claim "Ultimately, it's the omnipresence of the new police that has made the war undetectable" from page 12 of the Tiqqun collective's *Preliminary Materials for a Theory of the Young-Girl*, translated by Ariana Reines (Cambridge, MA: Semiotext(e), 2012).

"Scale Up" is for Fady Joudah.

Barniz de Pasto is a resin created by indigenous artists in the region now known as Colombia. Spanish colonizers conscripted local artists into using the resin to approximate objects of colonial desire, such as lacquered boxes from China and Japan. For a decolonial approach to this technique and its history, see the work of artist Nancy Friedemann-Sánchez.

The US military recognizes only the period between August 2, 1990 and February 28, 1991 as the conflict now known as the First Gulf War.

III.

Around 2015 I started to transcribe YouTube videos of self-styled alpha masters, men who fulfill the fetish role of humiliator and dominator for consenting customers. I expanded this transcription work to include amateur videos on pornography sites. Dom/sub sex can be many things, from abusive to liberating. My interest is in how masculine domination discourse overlaps with fascistic state logic. I'm thinking of far-right groups, such as the Proud Boys, that espouse domination of one's own desire as a foundation for domination of the household and eventually of the nation-state.

In the essay "Mama's Baby, Papa's Maybe: An American Grammar Book" (*Diacritics* 17, no. 2 [Summer 1987]: 64–81), Hortense Spillers theorizes Blackness and racialization through a gap between flesh and skin. "Video Tryouts for an American Grammar Book" tries to think about non-Black relations to that gap.

Vimeo.com hosts Tim Hetherington's video "Sleeping Soldiers," recorded in 2007–8 as he followed a US airborne infantry platoon in Afghanistan's Korengal Valley.

For a discussion of Etel Adnan's voice in a video recorded by the Otolith Group, see Anne Lesley Selcer, *Blank Sign Book* (Oakland, CA: Wolfman Books, 2019), 35–38.

A video of poet Jorie Graham's lecture "On Description," in which she speaks to the possibilities of sequencing sensory details in poetry, can be found on YouTube.

Edward Kienholz (1927–94) was an assemblage sculptor and installation artist.

"To One's Honor" mostly follows a modified hemistich meter in which the phrases on each side of the caesuras match in syllable count but the stress placement remains variable.

IV.

"Women imitate the earth" is a quotation from Plato on mimesis; see Elin Diamond, *Unmaking Mimesis: Essays on Feminism and Theatre* (London: Routledge, 1997), x.

"Like Daniel's prints saying *freedom / without love*" references a piece from Daniel

Joseph Martinez's *If Only God Had Invented Coca Cola, Sooner! Or, The Death of My Pet Monkey* (2004). This work is part of the permanent collection at the Museum of Modern Art in New York.

According to one of several versions of the Incan creation myth, Ayar Manco (later known as Manco Cápac) founded the capital Cuzco after sinking a golden staff provided by Viracocha, the creator god, into fertile soil.

The Magnificat, Mary's hymn of praise, is so called because she "magnifies" the Lord both in her soul's devotional song and in her bearing of the child Jesus. It is unique to the Gospel of Luke (1:46–55), and it contains the statement "He has filled the hungry with good things."